CULTURE IN ACTION

Writing a Screenplay

Liz Miles

Raintree

Chicago, Illinois

www.heinemannraintree.com
Visit our website to find out
more information about
Heinemann-Raintree books.

To order:
☎ Phone 888-454-2279
💻 Visit www.heinemannraintree.com
to browse our catalog and order online.

Edited by Louise Galpine and Rachel Howells
Designed by Kimberly Miracle and Betsy Wernert
Original illustrations © Capstone Global Library Ltd
Illustrated by kja-artists.com
Picture research by Mica Brancic and Kay Altwegg
Production by Alison Parsons
Originated by Steve Walker, Capstone Global Library Ltd
Printed in China by Leo Paper Products Ltd

13 12 11 10
10 9 8 7 6 5 4 3 2

Library of Congress Cataloging-in-Publication Data
Miles, Liz.
  Writing a screenplay / Liz Miles.
    p. cm. -- (Culture in action)
  Includes bibliographical references and index.
  ISBN 978-1-4109-3407-9 -- ISBN 978-1-4109-3424-6 (pbk.)
1. Motion picture authorship. I. Title.
  PN1996.M615 2009
  808.2'3--dc22
                        2008054328

Acknowledgments

The author and publishers are grateful to the following
for permission to reproduce copyright material: Alamy
p. **28** (Jim West); Getty Images pp. **18** (Michael Ochs
Archives), **26** (Vince Bucci); Rex Features pp. **4** (Everett/©
W. Disney), **6** (Everett/© 20th Century Fox), **7** (Everett
Collection), **8** (Humberto Carreno), **9** (Everett Collection),
19 (Everett/© 20th Century Fox), **20** (Everett/W. Disney), **21**
(Everett Collection), **27** (Everett/© BuenaVista), **29** (David
Fisher); The Kobal Collection pp. **5** (Jonathan Wenk), **10**
(Nickelodeon Movies), **11** (Warner Bros/DC Comics), **12**
(20th Century Fox), **15** (Universal Studios/Sophie Giraud), **16**
(Universal/Richard Cartwright), **22** (Castle Rock/Shangri-La
Entertainment), **23** (Universal City Studios/Rhythm & Blues).

Icon and banner images supplied by Shutterstock: © Alexander
Lukin, © ornitopter, © Colorlife, and © David S. Rose.

Cover photograph of a still from the film *Journey to the
Center of the Earth* reproduced with permission of The Kobal
Collection (New Line Cinema).

We would like to thank George Zwierzynski Jr., Jackie Murphy,
and Nancy Harris for their invaluable help in the preparation
of this book.

Every effort has been made to contact copyright holders
of material reproduced in this book. Any omissions will
be rectified in subsequent printings if notice is given to
the publishers.

All the Internet addresses (URLs) given in this book were valid
at the time of going to press. However, due to the dynamic
nature of the Internet, some addresses may have changed, or
sites may have changed or ceased to exist since publication.
While the author and publishers regret any inconvenience this
may cause readers, no responsibility for any such changes can
be accepted by either the author or the publishers.

Contents

Some words are printed in bold, **like this**. You can find out what they mean by looking in the glossary on page 30.

What Is a Screenplay?

Most television programs and movies start life as a screenplay or script. Whether it is for television or film, the actors need to know what the characters they are playing will say and do. Similarly, the **director** and other members of the team need instructions. For example, the director needs to know where a movie takes place.

What's in a screenplay?

A screenplay includes:

- character descriptions
- countries or rooms
- **dialogue**—what characters say and the noises they make
- acting and camera directions
- **special effects**—such as explosions or car chases
- sound effects/music.

Here are the stars of *High School Musical 3*. The screenplay for this movie also includes songs.

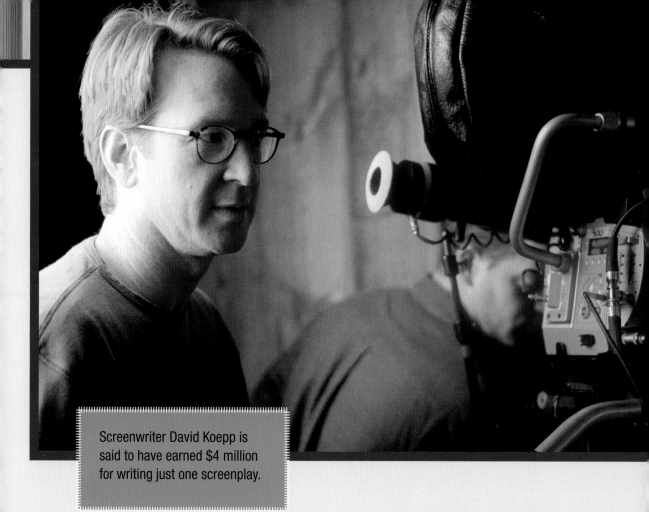

Screenwriter David Koepp is said to have earned $4 million for writing just one screenplay.

The root of the idea

The people who write screenplays are called screenwriters. A screenwriter starts with an idea. The idea may be original. Television **soap operas**, for example, are usually based on a new idea. Many screenplays are an **adaptation**—they are based on a work that already exists, such as a comic book or novel. Many scripts are the result of collaboration. Collaboration is when a team of writers work together to write and revise a script.

Guess who?

Even the best screenwriters often go unnoticed. For example, you may have heard of movies such as *Jurassic Park* (1993) and *Spider-Man* (2002), but do you know who wrote the scripts? In fact, David Koepp wrote the scripts. He is a very successful screenwriter.

All Kinds of Screenplays

A vast range of screenplays are written for the worlds of film and television. Each type of screenplay needs different writing skills and is targeted at a different audience. They vary from long movies about disasters for adults, such as *Titanic* (1997), to funny cartoons for children, such as *Scooby Doo*.

The audience and the **budget** for a movie may be much bigger than for a television program. This means that a movie screenwriter can include more costly actors and **locations** than the writer of a cheaper television series.

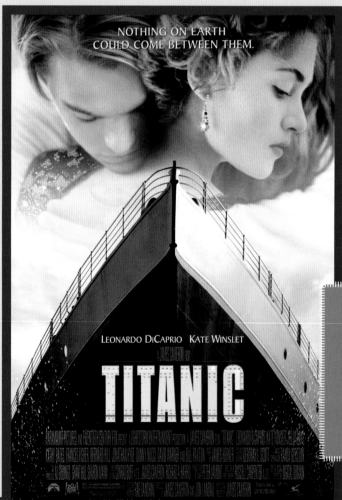

Titanic had a big budget of $200 million. This meant that the screenwriter could include lots of scenes that were expensive to make.

Some television programs last for years. The first series of *Scooby Doo* was shown in 1969!

A series or one-off?

A movie series is a number of movies that have similar characters and/or settings. Each of the movies is a complete story and stands alone. An example of this is the *Spider-Man* movie series.

A series for television is a number of programs, called episodes, that follow lengthy **plots**. In some types of series, such as **soap operas**, the screenwriters include **cliff-hangers** at the end of each episode. They hope that an exciting ending will make the audience want to watch the next episode. A soap can last for many years. *Guiding Light*, a popular U.S. soap opera, ran from 1937 to 2009.

High School Musical 2

The Disney cable television movie *High School Musical 2* first aired on August 17, 2007. It had an audience of 17 million, more viewers than any single cable television show in history.

Original or adaptation?

Screenplays can be an original work or an **adaptation**. An original screenplay is based on a new idea. An adaptation is based on already-published material, which can range from a novel to a comic. How close an adaptation is to the published material varies. For example, some fans of the Harry Potter books complain about the changes they have noticed in the movie adaptations.

From page to screen

To change a novel into a screenplay is a complicated job. Everything that happens has to come through **dialogue** and visual action. One screenwriting rule is "Show it, don't say it." There is rarely a narrator's voice to tell you what is happening or what people are thinking.

Lasting characters

Screenplays are often based on interesting characters that were invented in the past. Several movie screenplays, for example, have been written about Batman and Spider-Man. These characters first appeared in comics in 1939 and 1962.

This shot is from *Spider-Man 3* (2007). The superhero appears in a lot of screenplays—for movies, a TV action series, and animated cartoons.

New characters are often created for a new series or movie. They can become hugely popular. The comical, animated characters in *The Simpsons* first appeared in a series of short films in 1987. Soon the show was made into a half-hour episode. Since then, there have been more than 440 episodes of *The Simpsons*.

Period dramas

Classic novels are often adapted into period dramas for television and film. (A period drama is a story set in the past.) Screenwriters who adapt a novel, such as Jane Austen's *Pride and Prejudice*, must update dialogue that was written nearly 200 years ago for today's audiences to enjoy.

This period drama is an adaptation of a book. The television series has the same title as the book: *Pride and Prejudice*, written nearly 200 years ago.

What's Your Story?

The most important part of a script is the **plot**, or story. A good plot captures the audience's interest from the start and then holds its attention to the end.

The essentials

A good plot should include:

- Characters and setting: The main character or characters should be introduced right away. The screenwriter must make the viewer care about what happens to them and what they will do. The setting must be believable enough to seem real.

- Problem: A problem for the main character should appear. The problem is the "dramatic conflict" that provides the drama, or action. It pushes the character into action to seek an answer.

- Climax: The character struggles to find a solution. The climax could be a showdown, a car chase, or a battle.

- The resolution: The answer to the problem provides the ending. It should be believable and satisfying for the audience.

In *The Spiderwick Chronicles* (2008) the problem is a book that brings goblins to life. The climax is a battle with goblins.

Superman Returns (2006) uses a flashback to tell the backstory of how the hero first realized he could fly.

Backstory

A plot covers a specific period of time and often starts at a certain point in a character's life. A **backstory** is made up of the events that come before the period covered. For example, Batman's backstory is how he witnessed the murder of his parents and grew up determined to fight crime.

A backstory sometimes appears through flashbacks, dream sequences, or **dialogue**. However, too much backstory can bore an audience.

Subplots

A subplot is a less important story that happens alongside the main story. There can be more than one. A subplot can provide depth, variety, and extra action. In *Batman* movies, romance subplots in the superhero's life provide a change from the action.

Series plotting

A television series such as a **soap opera** needs a lot of dramatic conflicts that run together. Each conflict has to be resolved in a different episode. This can hold an audience's interest for weeks, or even months. Screenplays that have several plots need a team of 10 or more writers.

Cliff-hangers can draw vast audiences. In the television series *Dallas* (1980), a character called J.R. was injured. "Who shot J.R.?" was discussed in many magazines and talk shows.

Comedy

The drama in a comedy plot comes from characters' shock, surprise, bewilderment, and awkwardness. Often, the humor is in seeing adults behave like children. In *Home Alone* (1990), for example, the bumbling burglars who try to invade Kevin's home while his parents are away on vacation are very childlike.

In *Home Alone*, the long screams from eight-year-old Kevin make the audience laugh rather than shake with fear.

Setting the mood

A screenplay might include ideas for **incidental music** or the theme music at the beginning of a movie or TV program. The music may have an important connection to the subject of the movie, or the **lyrics** might provide information the writer wants the audience to hear.

Imagine you are a screenwriter for a television series. You have been asked to find a new theme tune. A theme tune is the music played at the start and end of a program.

Steps to follow:

1. Choose from:

   a) a **sitcom** such as *Hannah Montana*

   b) a **sci-fi** (science fiction) series, such as *Star Trek*

   c) a series of your own invention.

2. Look for a section of music that would suit the mood—funny, sad, or frightening.

Listen to a range of music, such as classical and pop, to find a tune that is memorable. This will help viewers recognize the television series when the music starts.

3. Think about the following during your search:

   a) How do you want the listener to feel when they hear the music?

   b) Do you want your music to appeal to adults or children, or both?

4. Play your choices to friends, and then discuss them. Describe the type of music you have chosen, and why.

Parts of a Screenplay

There are many different parts to a screenplay, and they are all laid out in a certain way. This makes it easy for **directors**, actors, actresses, and others to find what they are looking for quickly. Right away, they can see which parts are **dialogue** and which are directions. Each page of a screenplay is usually equal to around one minute of screen time when the movie or program is finished.

1

112 EXT—DAY

(The entrance to a cave. ELLA and ADAM walking into cave. Ella looking at a map.)

ELLA **6**

This way. This is the cave.

CUT TO: **4**

8 113 INT—DARK CAVE

(The camera is watching a flickering green light coming toward the characters or camera from the back of the cave. A rustling coming from the light, getting louder.) **5**

ADAM tugs at ELLA's arm. **2**

ADAM

(whispers)

Come on! Let's get out of here!

ELLA

(sharply)

No. We're not going anywhere. **7**

We've got to stay and see him.

To ask our question.

3 (Close-up. The light shows the characters' faces. They are staring up at the source of the light.)

ADAM

(scared)

Its eyes. Look at its eyes!

(Tilt to show face of DRAGON, light beams from its bloodshot eyes, staring down at the characters.)

ELLA

Shhh. Don't talk like that. You'll upset him.

(Ella talks nervously, politely to DRAGON)

Sir, please can you help us?

1. *Scene description:* Shows where the scene is set and whether it is an interior (INT) or exterior (EXT) scene. It usually tells you if the scene is set during the day or night.

2. *Action description:* Describes the action of the scene and what the characters do.

3. *Camera instructions:* If a certain camera move or angle is essential to the **plot**, it should be included.

4. *"Fade in" and "cut to":* Instruct how softly or dramatically one scene should change to the next.

5. *Sound directions:* Special sounds or noises may be essential to the plot. Some are written in capital letters to show their importance.

6. *Character speaking:* The name of the character speaking.

7. *Dialogue:* The dialogue is all the words that the performers speak. Dialogue is indented (nearer the middle of the page) so that it is easy to find and follow. There may be instructions in brackets or in *italic* type to describe how the words should be spoken.

8. *Scene number:* Makes it easy to find a certain place in the screenplay. Scenes are often rehearsed and filmed out of order. For example, all indoor scenes may be done first if a **location** has been rented for a few days.

Each scene filmed for a movie starts with the "clack" of a clapboard. The information on the board and its "clack" are used to put all the scenes and sound recordings together later.

Stories in pictures

Visualizing a story is vital when writing a successful screenplay. You need to imagine how each scene will look as it is filmed. For example, a crowded outdoor scene, such as a battle, would need a wide-angle shot from the camera. A wide-angle means a wide area is seen all at once.

Camera directions often used are:

- Point of view (POV): A shot as if seen from a character's point of view.
- Close-up (CU): Shows detail, such as a character's face.
- Pullback (PB): When the camera pulls back, more of the scene comes into view.
- Cut to: This is a clean break from one scene to another.
- Fade out: The scene goes black.
- Fade in: A new scene comes out of the black.
- Dissolve: Change from one scene to another, without going to black.

Storyboard

Directors or screenwriters often sketch out a **storyboard** to help them. They draw each camera shot, showing what the camera sees, and even its angle. For example, if the camera is seeing what a mouse sees, it might be angled up from the floor.

This is a storyboard for a scary movie.

Camera eyes

Steps to follow:

1. Choose a simple short story (or write your own). Imagine you are planning a television **adaptation** of it.

2. Plan and draw a storyboard of five to 10 pictures. Pick the most important scenes for each picture. Remember to include the problem, or dramatic conflict, and resolution. What should be the focus for each scene? Will your picture show a close-up or a wide-angle view? Will it be from a character's point of view?

3. When you have finished the pictures, write a caption for each. Together, the captions will briefly tell the story.

Consider what the focus should be in each scene. For example, which character is the most important?

Here is an example of a well-known story, written in five captions:

1. Cinderella cannot go to the ball. (Dramatic conflict.)

2. A fairy godmother waves her wand.

3. The prince dances with Cinderella.

4. Cinderella leaves her glass slipper behind.

5. The slipper fits Cinderella. (Final resolution.)

Who and Where?

As we have seen, it is a main character's struggle that provides the dramatic action in a **plot**. This means that creating a character who is likely to face problems is a first step in writing a screenplay. The second step is thinking of a **location** or situation. A location could provide a character with a problem.

Comedy characters

Comic characters have been popular since the early days of motion pictures. Some of the earliest comedies focused on clownish characters. Charlie Chaplain's character "the Tramp" (a tramp is a homeless person) in the early 1900s was popular because people both laughed at and felt sorry for him.

The Tramp (middle) is always getting into trouble. He is a silly and childlike comedy character.

Characters in comedies are always facing problems. The adults are usually childish. They struggle with a world that is filled with possible disasters. For example, when a comedy character steps in a puddle, the puddle might turn out to be a deep, muddy hole.

The cast

Screenwriters supply a list of all the characters. Actors and actresses usually read a script before accepting a part in a movie or TV program.

How to create a character

To create a convincing character you need to know every detail about them. They need to be well-rounded and believable. Ask and answer a lot of questions about your characters! For example, what color is his or her hair? What books does he or she like to read? What would your character do if . . .?

This is a comic scene from *The Simpsons Movie* (2007). Every member of the Simpson family has a quirky character.

A hungry rat leads to a lot of trouble (and comedy) in *Ratatouille*.

Setting the scene

The location of a story is a vital part of it. Different locations add drama, atmosphere (the feeling of a place), variety, and comedy. A screenplay may include instructions, such as, "Thick fog covers the forest path ahead."

From sitting rooms to outer space

The setting must suit the **genre**. Television **soap operas** and **sitcoms** are usually set in everyday locations. This helps the viewers understand the problems the characters face. In contrast, a **sci-fi** drama needs a stranger setting, such as an alien planet.

Specific locations give the writer all kinds of opportunities for things to happen to the characters. The restaurant kitchen location in *Ratatouille* (2007) leads to a lot of funny events related to food.

Mood changes

A change of location adds to the drama or suspense. When the main character, Lyra, goes to the Arctic in *The Golden Compass* (2007), the bleak atmosphere adds to the suspense. If heroes or heroines are put in dangerous places, the audience worries about them more. Seeing two characters wrestle close to a cliff-edge is more worrying than seeing them wrestle on a sofa.

How much does it cost?

Of course, the choice of location affects the cost of a movie or television program. Although **special effects** mean that just about any location is possible, faraway locations are very expensive. Usually, television programs have to cost less than movies. This means that television scripts are often set in everyday locations, and faraway locations are faked on a studio set.

Characters in *The Golden Compass* struggle to survive in the Arctic. The cold, bleak setting adds to the tension.

It's All Talk

Dialogue is all the words characters speak in a movie or fictional television program. A screenwriter uses dialogue to reveal the characters, move the story along, and provide information.

Choice of words

The words a character uses can reveal a lot. Using long words might suggest they are well-educated. Using a lot of slang (informal words) might suggest they are streetwise. Using the word *cool* to mean "good" is using slang.

There is not a lot of dialogue in *The Polar Express*, but nearly every sentence tells us something important.

How characters interact

How characters talk also tells viewers a lot. In *The Polar Express* (2004), one boy is very quiet. He is not excited about Christmas and does not want to see Santa. He wants to be alone and says, "Christmas just doesn't work out for me. Never has."

The replies from the boy and girl show they feel sorry for him and show they are kind and caring: "But Christmas is such a wonderful, beautiful time." "… this is Christmas Eve. Don't stay here by yourself." "We'll go together."

Backstory and plot

Because there is usually no narrator to tell us what has happened or is going to happen, the dialogue needs to keep the **plot** moving. The movie *Harry Potter and the Chamber of Secrets* (2002) opens with a visit from an elf named Dobby, who tells Harry: "Harry Potter must not go back to Hogwarts School of Witchcraft and Wizardry this year." This is **backstory** (see page 11). It tells us that Harry has been to this school already. Dobby then moves the plot along: "If Harry Potter goes back to school he will be in great danger." We now know that Harry Potter is probably going to be in danger because we are pretty sure he *will* go back to school!

In screenplays, words can come from the mouths of anyone or anything: elves, giants, and mermaids! In *Babe* (1995), the "star" pig says a lot of funny things.

Subtext

Often, there is an important meaning or feeling behind what a character says. This is called the subtext. Sometimes, a character can say one thing, but mean something very different. The character might avoid a subject altogether. Sometimes what characters do not say (the subtext) is more telling than what they do say.

JAMAL
Wow! We can make money.
Lots! Just think! A talking duck!
This is going to make us rich!
ANNA
People won't believe it.
Dad won't believe a duck can speak.
Anyway, he hates ducks.
JAMAL
Oh come on. Let's try.
This duck is great at telling jokes.
He'll make us famous. We'll be rich!
ANNA
(turns to Dave, the duck)
I'm not sure. Dave, what do you think?
DAVE, THE DUCK
Sure. I can make us rich!
I'd get a lot of laughs. But just one thing …
some people eat ducks, don't they?
JAMAL
No one will eat a funny duck!
You'll be the safest duck in the world. A star.
So let's sell tickets for a show on Saturday.
We'll put up posters. Dave, you'd better
start rehearsing.

Reveals character:
Short phrases show a character's excitement or fear.

Reveals character:
This shows what a character thinks about the situation.

Information:
This gives us extra details about the situation.

Backstory:
Background information is important for this plot.

Subtext:
Although the words suggest the character is brave, the pause suggests he is just trying to be brave, when in fact he is scared.

Plot:
A sentence like this one moves the story along.

Camera rolling

Write and perform your own script. You can work alone by writing a **monologue**. A monologue is one person talking or thinking out loud. If you want to work with friends, write a scene using dialogue for two or three characters. Dialogue is all the words that characters speak.

You could choose from the following:

- A lonely animal is planning an escape from a zoo (monologue in an animated movie).

- A young explorer has discovered a dragon in a cave (dialogue for a fantasy adventure movie).

- A girl or boy gets home late from school and must explain why to her or his parents (dialogue for a **sitcom**).

Plan your script by thinking about these questions:

- What is the plot? What is the backstory?

- What are the characters like? How are they feeling?

- What do the characters want to happen next? Will anything they say or do change things?

- What will you make happen next?

Keep your dialogue short and simple, especially for dramatic scenes such as this!

Read your script out loud as you write it. Does it sound natural? When acting your script, try different expressions and tones of voice.

The Best!

Screenwriters are often not well known. It is the **directors**, actors, and actresses who get all the attention. However, a few screenwriters have become famous names, such as Mike Leigh and Woody Allen. This is partly because they are successful directors, too!

It is hard to become a successful screenwriter. Film and television companies usually rely on the writers they already know for blockbuster movies or big-**budget** dramas. Here is a list of some great screenwriters:

Peter Jackson

Jackson is a movie director, producer (person who organizes the money needed to make a movie), and screenwriter. He worked on the *Lord of the Rings* movies (2001–03) and *King Kong* (2005).

Diablo Cody

Diablo Cody is a screenwriter who found great success very quickly. In 2007 she won the Academy Award for Best Original Screenplay for the movie *Juno*. It was the first screenplay she had ever written!

Diablo Cody is a U.S. screenwriter. She won an Oscar for Best Original Screenplay for *Juno* in 2007.

The funny and exciting screenplays for the *Pirates of the Caribbean* movies were a team effort—written by two men named Terry and Ted.

Brad Bird

Many screenwriters are multitalented. Brad Bird is an Oscar-winning director, as well as a screenwriter and actor in *The Incredibles* (2004) and *Ratatouille* (2007).

Terry and Ted

Screenwriters often work in pairs. This is the case with duo Terry Rossio and Ted Elliott. Together they wrote the screenplay for *Aladdin* (1992) and the *Pirates of the Caribbean* movies.

Andrew Davies

Davies is one of the best-known television screenwriters. He is admired for his **adaptations** of novels that were written in the past, such as *Pride and Prejudice* by Jane Austen. He adapts the stories so that modern audiences can easily enjoy them.

First Steps to Success

Many people hope to follow in the footsteps of some of the big names in screenwriting. An award for a great television series or an award for best original screenplay may also be their goal.

First stage

Writing short scenes is a good way to start. Joining a writing group or club, and working with other writers is helpful, too. Practice is essential, as even the most skilled screenwriters rewrite and revise their work over and over again.

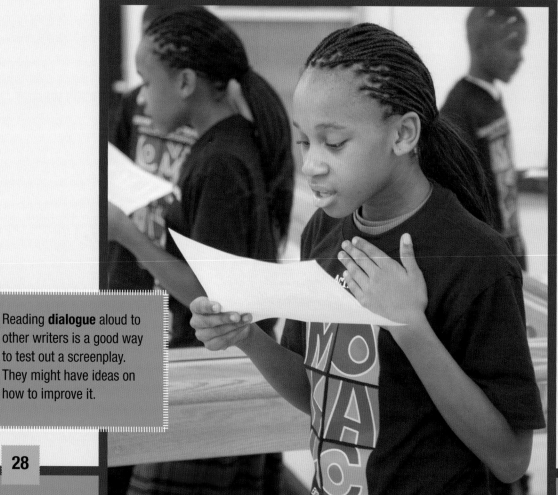

Reading **dialogue** aloud to other writers is a good way to test out a screenplay. They might have ideas on how to improve it.

In 2007, 14-year-old Rosalind Peters won an award for her own movie, which she wrote and filmed. It is called *The Unwelcome Stranger*.

Learn from the experts

The only way to find out what makes a script successful is to study scripts by well-known writers. You can find free sample scripts on the Internet.

How to write for television

People often start writing for television by picking their favorite television series and writing an episode. Study the program first. Make notes about the characters, how they speak, and their stories so far. Then try writing a show.

How to write for the movies

Some top movie writers (and **directors**), such as Peter Jackson, found success by making their own short film. It is fairly easy to make a movie. You can use a digital video recorder, **video-editing program**, and computer. Even if the final movie is not perfect, it should show how good or bad the screenplay is. At least you will find out what needs to be improved.

Glossary

adaptation screenplay that is based on material that is already published. Shakespeare's plays are often adapted for television.

backstory events that have come before the time the story takes place

budget available money. A multimillion-dollar budget is common in the movie world, but rare for television programs.

cliff-hanger high point of suspense at the end of a television episode or series. A good cliff-hanger makes an audience want to watch the next episode.

dialogue words that actors speak

director person that controls how a movie or TV program is made. The director tells actors how each scene should be acted.

genre movie or program that has a certain type of content and form. Action is a genre that has a lot of special effects.

incidental music music that accompanies action or dialogue. Creepy incidental music adds suspense to a horror movie.

location where movie or TV programs are filmed. "On location" means that the filming is done outside the studio.

lyrics words sung to music

monologue one person talking or thinking out loud

plot main events in a story, movie, or TV program. A plot needs a clear beginning or problem, and a clear end or resolution.

sci-fi (short for science fiction) any story about the future or outer space. Sci-fi movies are often set in the future or involve spaceships and aliens.

sitcom situation-comedy series that puts everyday people in embarrassing or funny situations. *Friends* is one of the most popular sitcoms ever made.

soap opera series of episodes about fictional people and their everyday lives. Soap operas involve teams of screenwriters, who write many plots for numerous episodes.

special effects any events, characters, or settings that need stunts or computer-generated images. For example, the way a giant gorilla appears to jump over a burning building is created by using special effects.

storyboard sequence of images to show how scenes should look when they are filmed. Storyboards for animations show some of the pictures the animators will have to draw.

video-editing program computer software that helps you change what you have filmed. You can use this type of program to change the order of scenes and to add music or sounds.

Find Out More

Books

Hamilton, John. *Screenplay* (*Your Write It!*). Edina, Minn.: ABDO, 2009.

Mack, James. *Write for Success* (*Life Skills*). Chicago: Heinemann Library, 2009.

McAlpine, Margaret. *Working in Film and Television* (*My Future Career*). Milwaukee: Gareth Stevens, 2005.

Websites

Simply Scripts
www.simplyscripts.com
Download scripts for free to find out about some of the tools used by screenwriters in the past.

Film Street
www.filmstreet.co.uk
Search the library of adaptations, or submit a video of your own screenplay!

Index